TABLE OF CONTENT

Chapter 1: Understanding Mindfulness

•Definition of Mindfulness
Explanation of mindfulness as being fully present in the moment without judgment.
•Mindfulness vs. Meditation
Clarify the differences and connections between mindfulness and meditation.
•The Science Behind Mindfulness
Overview of research studies that demonstrate the mental, emotional, and physical benefits of mindfulness practices.
•Mindfulness in Daily Life
Discuss how mindfulness can be practiced throughout the day—while eating, walking, working, etc.

Chapter 2: The Benefits of Mindfulness

•Physical Benefits
How mindfulness can help reduce stress, lower blood pressure, and improve sleep quality.
•Emotional Benefits
Enhance emotional regulation, increase self-awareness, and reduce anxiety and depression.
•Cognitive Benefits
Improved focus, memory, and cognitive flexibility through regular mindfulness practice.
•Spiritual Benefits
Connecting mindfulness to a deeper sense of purpose and inner peace.

Chapter 3: Introduction to Meditation

•What is Meditation?
Definition and purpose of meditation as a formal practice of focusing the mind.
•Different Types of Meditation
Overview of meditation styles: mindfulness meditation, transcendental meditation, loving-kindness meditation, and more.
•Common Misconceptions About Meditation
Addressing myths like "meditation is hard" or "you need to clear your mind completely."

Chapter 4: Starting a Meditation Practice

•Setting the Stage for Meditation
How to create a peaceful environment for meditation: location, posture, and tools (cushions, music, incense).
•Finding Time to Meditate
How to build meditation into a busy schedule and develop a consistent practice.
•How Long to Meditate
Advice on session lengths, starting small, and gradually increasing meditation time.
•Guided vs. Silent Meditation
Discuss the differences and benefits of using guided meditations versus practicing in silence.

Chapter 5: Mindfulness Meditation Techniques

•The Body Scan
How to perform a body scan meditation to release tension and become aware of physical sensations.
•Breath Awareness
Using the breath as an anchor to the present moment, learning to focus on inhaling and exhaling.
•Noting and Labeling
Observing and naming thoughts or feelings without judgment as they arise during meditation.

•Loving-Kindness Meditation (Metta)
A guide to cultivating compassion for yourself and others through meditation.

Chapter 6: Overcoming Common Challenges in Meditation

•Restlessness and Fidgeting
Techniques for dealing with physical discomfort or the urge to move.
•Intrusive Thoughts
How to handle thoughts that arise during meditation without getting frustrated.
•Lack of Time
Practical tips for squeezing in mindfulness and meditation even on the busiest days.
•Impatience and Frustration
Overcoming the desire for quick results and learning to appreciate the slow, gradual benefits.

Chapter 7: Mindfulness Beyond Meditation

•Mindful Eating
How to practice mindfulness during meals, appreciating the sensory experience of food.
•Mindful Walking
Bringing mindfulness into daily walks by focusing on movement, breathing, and surroundings.
•Mindful Communication
Enhancing relationships by being fully present in conversations, listening actively, and responding thoughtfully.
•Mindfulness in Stressful Situations
Practical tips for staying calm and mindful when faced with challenges or conflicts.

Chapter 8: Mindfulness in Everyday Life

•Developing Mindful Habits

Tips for incorporating mindfulness into daily routines: mornings, work, evenings.
•Mindfulness for Focus and Productivity
How mindfulness can improve concentration, decision-making, and efficiency.
•Mindfulness for Emotional Balance
Techniques for responding to emotions mindfully, rather than reacting impulsively.

Chapter 9: Deepening Your Meditation Practice

•Building Consistency
How to stay motivated and committed to a long-term meditation practice.
•Exploring Advanced Techniques
Introduction to deeper meditative practices, including mantras, visualizations, and chakra meditation.
•Group Meditation and Retreats
The benefits of meditating in groups or attending meditation retreats for deeper exploration.

Chapter 10: The Long-Term Benefits of Mindfulness and Meditation

•Mindful Living as a Lifestyle
How mindfulness can transform not just moments, but entire ways of living.
•Emotional Resilience and Mental Clarity
The long-term effects of mindfulness on emotional stability and clear thinking.
•Spiritual Growth and Inner Peace
Exploring the deeper connection between mindfulness and personal spirituality.

Conclusion

•Embracing Mindfulness and Meditation for Life

Summarize the key takeaways of mindfulness and meditation and encourage readers to continue their journey.
•Final Thoughts
Motivation and inspiration for readers to incorporate mindfulness and meditation into their daily lives for long-term well-being.

CHAPTER ONE

In our increasingly hectic and fast-paced world, many of us are searching for ways to regain a sense of balance, calm, and clarity. The practices of mindfulness and meditation offer just that—a path to inner peace and mental well-being that has been embraced for thousands of years and is now backed by modern science. Whether you're new to these practices or looking to deepen your understanding, this book is designed to guide you through the essentials, helping you integrate mindfulness and meditation into your daily life.

Definition of Mindfulness
Mindfulness is the art of being fully present in the moment, paying attention to your thoughts, feelings, and sensations without judgment or distraction. It's about observing what's happening both inside and outside of you with a sense of curiosity rather than criticism. When we practice mindfulness, we are fully engaged in whatever we're doing—whether that's eating a meal, walking in nature, or having a conversation—without letting our mind wander to past regrets or future anxieties. The goal is not to avoid thoughts or emotions but to experience them with acceptance, cultivating a deeper awareness of ourselves and the world around us.

Mindfulness vs. Meditation
While mindfulness and meditation are often mentioned together, they are distinct yet complementary practices. **Mindfulness** is a state of being—an ongoing awareness that can be maintained throughout the day. It's something you practice in the moment, as

you go about your daily tasks, bringing your full attention to the present. **Meditation**, on the other hand, is a more structured, formal practice where you intentionally set aside time to quiet the mind and focus your attention. While mindfulness can be practiced throughout the day, meditation helps train the mind to become more mindful. Think of meditation as the exercise that strengthens your ability to live mindfully.

The Science Behind Mindfulness

The benefits of mindfulness are not just philosophical; they are grounded in science. Over the past few decades, researchers have explored the effects of mindfulness on the brain and body, uncovering compelling evidence that regular practice can improve mental, emotional, and physical health. Studies have shown that mindfulness reduces stress by lowering cortisol levels, the hormone associated with stress. It can enhance emotional regulation, helping individuals better manage anxiety, depression, and mood swings. Mindfulness has also been shown to improve focus and cognitive flexibility, and even lead to physical changes in the brain—specifically in areas responsible for attention, empathy, and emotional processing. The practice can also positively impact physical health, reducing blood pressure, improving sleep, and promoting overall well-being.

Mindfulness in Daily Life

One of the greatest strengths of mindfulness is that it can be practiced anytime, anywhere. You don't need to sit cross-legged in a quiet room to experience the benefits. Mindfulness can be seamlessly integrated into your daily routine. For example, **mindful eating** involves paying close attention to the textures, tastes, and sensations of each bite, rather than rushing through a meal. **Mindful walking** encourages you to focus on each step, the feel of the ground beneath your feet, and the rhythm of your breath. You can even practice **mindful communication** by being fully present in conversations—listening without interrupting, and responding with thoughtfulness rather than reacting automatically. The key is to bring awareness and presence to everyday moments, turning even mundane tasks into opportunities for mindfulness.

As you embark on this journey, you will discover how mindfulness and meditation can transform your relationship with yourself, others, and the world around you. Through these practices, you can cultivate greater peace, clarity, and resilience, allowing you to navigate life's challenges with a sense of calm and purpose.

CHAPTER TWO

The Benefits of Mindfulness

The practice of mindfulness offers a wide range of benefits that extend beyond just feeling more present and aware. As we immerse ourselves in mindfulness, we begin to see profound improvements in our physical, emotional, cognitive, and even spiritual well-being. In this chapter, we will explore how mindfulness can enhance various aspects of our lives, from reducing stress and anxiety to promoting a deeper sense of inner peace and purpose.

1. Physical Benefits

Mindfulness has a direct and positive impact on our physical health. By training ourselves to be more present and engaged in the moment, we can influence how our bodies respond to stress, improve sleep quality, and even lower blood pressure.

•Reducing Stress:
One of the most well-known benefits of mindfulness is its ability to reduce stress. When we practice mindfulness, we focus on the present rather than ruminating about the past or worrying about the future. This shift in attention helps to calm the mind and, in turn,

reduce the body's stress response. Research shows that mindfulness can lower cortisol levels, which is the hormone responsible for stress. By consistently engaging in mindfulness practices, you can decrease the body's fight-or-flight response, helping to alleviate chronic stress and its associated physical symptoms, such as headaches, muscle tension, and digestive issues.

•Lowering Blood Pressure:

Stress is a significant factor in high blood pressure, but mindfulness has been shown to help reduce this risk. When you practice mindfulness, particularly mindfulness meditation, you activate the body's relaxation response. This leads to improved blood circulation, slower heart rate, and a reduction in overall blood pressure levels. Over time, consistent mindfulness practice can help to manage and even lower high blood pressure, promoting cardiovascular health.

•Improving Sleep Quality:

Many people struggle with insomnia or restless sleep due to racing thoughts or unresolved stress. Mindfulness can significantly improve sleep quality by teaching us how to calm the mind before bed. Practices like body scan meditation or mindful breathing can help relax the body and mind, making it easier to fall asleep and stay asleep. By incorporating mindfulness into your nightly routine, you can create a peaceful transition from wakefulness to sleep, leading to more restful and restorative nights.

2. Emotional Benefits

Mindfulness is a powerful tool for emotional regulation. By becoming more aware of our thoughts and feelings, we learn how to respond to emotions mindfully rather than reacting impulsively. This awareness leads to greater emotional stability and an overall improvement in mental health.

•Enhancing Emotional Regulation:

One of the key emotional benefits of mindfulness is its ability to enhance emotional regulation. Mindfulness teaches us to observe our emotions as they arise without judgment or immediate reaction. Instead of being swept away by anger, sadness, or frustration, mindfulness helps us recognize these emotions, understand their root causes, and respond to them thoughtfully. This ability to regulate emotions is crucial in maintaining emotional balance and reducing the intensity of negative feelings.

•Reducing Anxiety and Depression:
Numerous studies have demonstrated that mindfulness can significantly reduce symptoms of anxiety and depression. By bringing attention to the present moment, mindfulness reduces overthinking and rumination, which are common triggers for both anxiety and depression. Additionally, mindfulness encourages self-compassion and acceptance, helping individuals feel more in control of their emotional state. Mindfulness-based therapies, such as Mindfulness-Based Stress Reduction (MBSR) and Mindfulness-Based Cognitive Therapy (MBCT), have been particularly effective in treating these conditions, offering a natural and sustainable way to manage mental health challenges.

•Increasing Self-Awareness:
A core component of mindfulness is self-awareness—becoming more in tune with our thoughts, behaviors, and emotions. This heightened awareness allows us to recognize patterns in our thoughts and actions, helping us understand why we react in certain ways and how we can make more mindful choices. Self-awareness is a key to personal growth, as it enables us to identify areas of improvement, challenge negative thought patterns, and cultivate more positive habits.

3. Cognitive Benefits

Mindfulness is not only beneficial for emotional well-being, but it also enhances cognitive functioning. Regular mindfulness practice has been shown to improve focus, memory, and overall mental clarity.

•Improved Focus and Concentration:
In our modern world, where distractions are abundant, the ability to focus and maintain concentration is invaluable. Mindfulness trains the brain to stay focused on the present moment, improving attention span and the ability to concentrate on tasks. This benefit extends to both work and personal life, helping you be more productive and efficient.
•Enhanced Memory:
Research suggests that mindfulness can improve both working memory (the ability to hold and manipulate information in your mind) and long-term memory. By reducing distractions and improving focus, mindfulness allows us to process information more effectively, leading to better memory retention. This cognitive benefit is particularly valuable for students, professionals, and anyone looking to sharpen their mental skills.
•Increased Cognitive Flexibility:
Cognitive flexibility refers to the brain's ability to adapt to new information, think creatively, and solve problems. Mindfulness helps enhance this flexibility by encouraging an open-minded and non-judgmental approach to thoughts and experiences. When we practice mindfulness, we become more adaptable and able to shift perspectives, making it easier to navigate challenges and come up with innovative solutions.

4. Spiritual Benefits

For many, mindfulness is more than just a tool for managing stress or enhancing focus; it is also a pathway to spiritual growth and a deeper connection to one's purpose in life. While mindfulness itself is not inherently spiritual, it can lead to a greater sense of peace, purpose, and understanding.

•Connecting to Inner Peace:
Mindfulness encourages us to quiet the mind and become more attuned to our inner world. By practicing mindfulness, we cultivate a

sense of inner peace that is not reliant on external circumstances. This peaceful state allows us to navigate life's ups and downs with greater ease, knowing that true peace comes from within.

•Cultivating a Deeper Sense of Purpose:

Through mindfulness, we can develop a clearer understanding of our values and goals, leading to a greater sense of purpose. By regularly checking in with ourselves, we become more in tune with what truly matters to us, which can help guide our decisions and actions in alignment with our deeper aspirations.

•Spiritual Awakening:

For some, mindfulness serves as a gateway to spiritual awakening—a realization of the interconnectedness of all things and a deeper sense of presence in the world. While mindfulness itself is not tied to any specific religion or belief system, it can foster a sense of unity and oneness, opening the door to profound spiritual insights.

As we have seen, mindfulness offers an incredible range of benefits that touch on every aspect of our lives—physical, emotional, cognitive, and spiritual. Whether you're looking to reduce stress, improve focus, or connect with a deeper sense of peace, mindfulness provides the tools needed to transform both your inner and outer world. In the next chapter, we will explore the practice of meditation, which serves as a powerful foundation for cultivating mindfulness and deepening these benefits.

CHAPTER THREE

Introduction to Meditation

Meditation is often considered the foundation of mindfulness practices, providing a structured approach to cultivating awareness and mental clarity. While mindfulness can be practiced throughout daily activities, meditation offers a formal and focused way to train the mind. In this chapter, we will explore what meditation is, the various types of meditation, and common misconceptions that often prevent people from starting or maintaining a practice.

What is Meditation?

At its core, meditation is a formal practice of focusing the mind, with the purpose of achieving a heightened state of awareness, mental clarity, and inner calm. While there are many different forms of meditation, they all share the common goal of training the mind to concentrate, remain present, and eventually transcend the distractions of everyday thought patterns.

Meditation often involves sitting quietly in a comfortable position, closing the eyes, and focusing on a specific object of attention—such as the breath, a mantra, or a visual image. By continuously redirecting the mind to this point of focus, meditation helps quiet mental chatter and cultivate a sense of stillness. Over time, with consistent practice, meditation allows us to become more aware of our thoughts and emotions, and less reactive to them. This practice not only enhances mental clarity but also fosters emotional balance and a deeper sense of peace.

While the ultimate purpose of meditation varies from tradition to tradition, it is widely recognized as a tool for improving overall well-being, reducing stress, and enhancing focus. For some, meditation is also a means of deepening spiritual insight and connection.

Different Types of Meditation

Meditation is not a one-size-fits-all practice. There are many styles and approaches, each offering unique benefits and experiences. Here are some of the most common types of meditation:

•Mindfulness Meditation:
Mindfulness meditation is one of the most widely practiced forms in the modern world, often associated with secular mindfulness practices. The focus here is on cultivating present-moment awareness by observing thoughts, sensations, and emotions without judgment. In mindfulness meditation, the practitioner usually focuses on the breath or bodily sensations while allowing thoughts to arise and pass without getting caught up in them. The goal is not to stop thinking but to become more aware of thought patterns and how they influence emotions and actions.

•Transcendental Meditation (TM):
Transcendental Meditation is a specific technique that involves silently repeating a mantra (a word, sound, or phrase) for 20 minutes, twice a day. TM is designed to help the mind settle into a state of restful alertness, allowing deeper relaxation and stress reduction. Unlike mindfulness meditation, which encourages awareness of the present moment, TM emphasizes going beyond (or "transcending") thoughts and achieving a state of pure consciousness. This form of meditation is widely practiced for its stress-relieving and clarity-enhancing benefits.

•Loving-Kindness Meditation (Metta):
Loving-kindness meditation, or Metta meditation, is a practice focused on cultivating compassion and love for oneself and others. In this meditation, the practitioner silently repeats phrases of goodwill, such as "May I be happy. May I be healthy. May I be at peace." After starting with oneself, the practitioner extends these wishes to others, including loved ones, acquaintances, and even those with whom they have conflict. Loving-kindness meditation is particularly effective for fostering emotional resilience, increasing empathy, and reducing negative emotions like anger and resentment.

•Guided Meditation:
Guided meditation involves listening to a recorded or live guide who leads the practitioner through a specific meditation experience. This might include visualizations, body scans, or guided breathing exercises. Guided meditations are especially helpful for beginners

who may need direction and structure as they develop their practice. Many people find that listening to a calming voice or following a structured path makes it easier to relax and stay focused.

    •Body Scan Meditation:

In body scan meditation, the focus is on scanning the body for sensations, often starting at the feet and moving up toward the head. This practice helps to cultivate greater body awareness and is commonly used for relaxation and releasing physical tension. It's particularly beneficial for those looking to reconnect with their bodies and manage stress or discomfort.

    •Zen Meditation (Zazen):

Zen meditation, also known as Zazen, is rooted in Buddhist tradition and typically involves sitting in a specific posture and focusing on the breath or observing thoughts without attachment. In Zen practice, the goal is not to control or stop thoughts but to develop an awareness that transcends the busy mind. Zen meditation is often more formal, requiring consistent dedication and focus on maintaining the posture and stillness of the body.

These are just a few examples of the many styles of meditation available. Each type offers its own benefits, and many people experiment with different methods before finding the one that resonates best with them. Regardless of the style you choose, the key is to commit to the practice and allow it to unfold naturally over time.

Common Misconceptions About Meditation

Despite its growing popularity, many myths and misconceptions about meditation persist, preventing people from embracing the practice. Let's address some of the most common misunderstandings:

    •"Meditation is hard."

One of the biggest misconceptions is that meditation is difficult or requires a lot of skill. In reality, meditation is a practice that anyone can begin, regardless of experience. Like any new habit, it may feel challenging at first, but the key is to approach it with patience and persistence. The practice isn't about getting it "right" or achieving immediate results. It's about showing up, sitting quietly, and allowing your mind to settle over time. Even a few minutes a day can make a difference.

•"You need to clear your mind completely."
Many people believe that meditation requires clearing the mind of all thoughts, which can be intimidating and discouraging. However, meditation is not about eliminating thoughts but rather learning to observe them without attachment. Thoughts are a natural part of the mind, and they will inevitably arise during meditation. The goal is to acknowledge them without judgment and gently return your focus to your point of attention, whether that's the breath, a mantra, or a visual image. Over time, this practice helps to quiet the mind, but there's no need to force it.

•"I don't have time to meditate."
Another common misconception is that meditation requires large blocks of time to be effective. While longer sessions can deepen the experience, even just a few minutes of meditation each day can have noticeable benefits. The most important aspect of meditation is consistency, not duration. Starting with five or ten minutes a day and gradually building up as your practice develops is a realistic and manageable way to integrate meditation into a busy schedule.

•"Meditation is only for spiritual or religious people."
While meditation has roots in many spiritual traditions, it is not inherently religious. In fact, meditation can be practiced by anyone, regardless of their beliefs. Many modern meditation techniques, especially mindfulness meditation, are entirely secular and focus on improving mental clarity, emotional balance, and well-being. Whether you are seeking spiritual insight or simply want to reduce stress and improve focus, meditation offers something for everyone.

•"You need to sit in a certain way to meditate."
While many images of meditation show people sitting cross-legged on the floor, it's not necessary to adopt any specific posture to

meditate. The most important thing is that you are comfortable and can maintain your position without strain. Whether you sit in a chair, lie down, or even walk mindfully, meditation is about finding what works best for you. As long as you can focus your attention and remain present, you are meditating.

By addressing these misconceptions, we can break down the barriers that often prevent people from trying meditation. The truth is, meditation is a simple yet powerful practice that anyone can benefit from. With the right mindset and a willingness to begin, you can experience the transformative effects of meditation in your daily life.

Meditation, like mindfulness, offers a way to connect more deeply with the present moment, cultivate mental clarity, and foster a greater sense of peace. As we've explored in this chapter, meditation is accessible to everyone, regardless of experience, time constraints, or background. In the following chapter, we will guide you through the steps to begin your own meditation practice, helping you set the stage for a consistent and fulfilling journey into mindfulness and meditation.

CHAPTER FOUR
Starting a Meditation Practice

Now that you understand the basics of mindfulness and meditation, it's time to explore how to start your own meditation practice. Creating an environment that fosters focus and relaxation, finding time in your day to meditate, and understanding different approaches will help you build a consistent and rewarding routine. This chapter will guide you through the key elements of getting started: setting the stage, finding time, choosing the right session length, and understanding the differences between guided and silent meditation.

Creating the right environment for meditation is essential to cultivate a peaceful and mindful practice. While you don't need an elaborate setup, there are a few factors that can enhance your meditation experience, allowing you to feel more centered and present.

- Location:

Choose a quiet, comfortable space where you can sit undisturbed for the duration of your meditation. This could be a corner of your bedroom, a dedicated meditation room, or even a quiet spot outdoors. The key is to find a place where distractions are minimal, and you feel calm and relaxed. If possible, designate this spot solely for meditation to create a mental association with peace and focus.

- Posture:

Posture plays an important role in meditation, as it helps to keep you alert and comfortable. You don't have to sit cross-legged on the floor, but maintaining an upright posture is important for staying engaged and focused. Sit on a cushion or a chair with your feet flat on the ground, your spine straight, and your hands resting gently on your lap or knees. Keep your shoulders relaxed and your head balanced naturally on your neck. If sitting is uncomfortable for long periods, you can also try meditating while lying down, but be mindful of the tendency to fall asleep in this position.

•Tools:

While meditation doesn't require any specific tools, certain items can enhance the experience:

•Cushions: Sitting on a cushion (or a meditation-specific pillow called a "zafu") can help you maintain proper posture and prevent discomfort, especially during longer sessions.

•Music: Some people find that soft, ambient music or nature sounds help create a calming atmosphere. Instrumental music without lyrics works best, as it won't distract you from your focus.

•Incense or Candles: Scent can be a powerful tool for creating a meditative space. Lighting incense or a candle can provide a sensory cue that it's time to meditate, helping to shift your mind into a state of relaxation and focus. Choose scents like lavender, sandalwood, or frankincense for their calming properties.

Setting the stage for meditation doesn't have to be complicated. The most important thing is that you feel comfortable and at ease in your space, allowing you to focus inward without distraction.

2. Finding Time to Meditate

In today's busy world, finding time to meditate can seem like a challenge. However, the beauty of meditation is that it can fit into even the busiest schedule. Consistency is more important than the length of time you spend meditating, so even a few minutes a day can make a difference.

•Start Small:
If you're new to meditation, start with short sessions—5 to 10 minutes is a good place to begin. Gradually increase the duration as you become more comfortable with the practice. Short, frequent sessions are better than infrequent, long ones, as they help establish a consistent routine without feeling overwhelming.
•Integrate Meditation into Daily Routines:
Look for natural pockets of time in your day where you can fit in meditation. For example, you might meditate first thing in the morning to set a calm and focused tone for the day. Alternatively, you could meditate during a lunch break or right before bed to unwind. The key is to choose a time when you're unlikely to be interrupted, allowing you to fully engage with the practice.
•Be Flexible:
Life is unpredictable, and there will be days when sticking to a strict meditation schedule is difficult. Instead of being rigid, allow yourself the flexibility to adjust. If you only have a few minutes on certain days, that's fine—what matters most is your commitment to showing up, even briefly. On busier days, you can also practice informal mindfulness throughout your activities, such as mindful breathing or walking.

•Make It a Habit:
To develop consistency, it can be helpful to link meditation to an existing habit, such as brushing your teeth or making your morning coffee. By attaching your meditation practice to something you already do, it becomes easier to build the habit over time.

3. How Long to Meditate

The ideal length of a meditation session varies from person to person and can evolve as your practice deepens. When you're starting out, it's more important to focus on consistency rather than session length. Here are some guidelines to help you determine how long to meditate:

•Start Small:
If you're a beginner, start with short sessions—around 5 to 10 minutes. This gives you time to settle into the practice without feeling overwhelmed or restless. As you become more comfortable, gradually extend the time in 5-minute increments. Aim to work up to 20 minutes, which is a commonly recommended duration for daily practice.
•Listen to Your Body and Mind:
Meditation is about being in tune with yourself, so it's important to listen to how you're feeling during your sessions. If you find yourself becoming restless or unfocused after 10 minutes, it's perfectly fine to stop there. Over time, as your focus and patience increase, you may find that longer sessions feel more natural and fulfilling.
•Set Realistic Goals:
Avoid the temptation to push yourself into long sessions too quickly. Meditation is not about endurance—it's about quality of attention. It's better to have a focused 10-minute session than a distracted 30-minute one. As you progress, you may find that meditating for 15 to 30 minutes is enough to bring noticeable benefits to your mental clarity and emotional balance.

There are two main approaches to meditation: guided and silent. Both have their advantages, and the best option for you will depend on your preferences and experience level.

•Guided Meditation:

In guided meditation, an instructor (either live or through a recording) leads you through the meditation process. This may include verbal instructions, visualizations, breathing techniques, or mindfulness cues. Guided meditations are especially helpful for beginners, as they provide structure and direction, making it easier to stay focused. Many people also find guided meditations to be more relaxing, as they don't have to rely solely on their own mental discipline. There are numerous apps and online resources offering guided meditations on a variety of themes, from relaxation to mindfulness to self-compassion.

•Silent Meditation:

In silent meditation, there is no external guidance—just you and your breath, or another point of focus, such as a mantra or a body scan. Silent meditation requires more mental discipline and may feel challenging at first, but it offers the opportunity for deeper introspection and self-awareness. Without the distraction of a guide, you are fully responsible for maintaining your attention and bringing yourself back to the present moment when your mind wanders. Silent meditation can lead to profound insights and a greater connection with your inner self, but it often takes time and practice to feel comfortable with the stillness.

•Which One to Choose?

If you're new to meditation, starting with guided sessions can be a helpful way to build your practice. As you gain confidence, you might experiment with silent meditation to develop more independence and deepen your focus. Many experienced meditators use a combination of both, depending on their needs and mood. For example, you might use guided meditations during particularly stressful times when it's harder to focus, and silent meditation when you're feeling more centered.

Starting a meditation practice doesn't have to be complicated. By creating a peaceful space, setting realistic goals, and exploring different approaches, you can build a routine that fits your lifestyle and needs. Remember, meditation is a personal journey, and there's no right or wrong way to do it. The most important thing is to start, and with time, you'll discover the immense benefits that meditation can bring to your mind, body, and spirit.

CHAPTER FIVE

Mindfulness Meditation Techniques

In this chapter, we will explore four essential mindfulness meditation techniques that help you deepen your practice, release tension, and cultivate self-awareness and compassion. Each technique offers a unique approach to focusing the mind, grounding yourself in the present, and nurturing a sense of inner peace. Whether you're a beginner or an experienced practitioner, these techniques will serve as valuable tools in your mindfulness and meditation journey.

The Body Scan

The body scan meditation is a powerful practice for releasing tension and becoming more aware of the physical sensations in your body. It encourages you to pay close attention to each part of your body, helping you connect with how you're feeling physically and mentally. This practice is especially useful for identifying areas of tension or discomfort that you might not be consciously aware of.

How to Perform a Body Scan Meditation:

1.   Find a comfortable position:
You can lie down on your back, sit in a chair, or sit cross-legged on the floor. Close your eyes and take a few deep breaths to relax.

2.   Begin at the top of your head:
Start by bringing your attention to the top of your head. Notice any sensations—whether it's tension, relaxation, or even neutrality. There's no need to change anything, just observe.
3.   Move down through your body:
Slowly move your attention downward, scanning your body from head to toe. Bring awareness to your forehead, eyes, jaw, neck, shoulders, and down through your arms, chest, abdomen, hips, legs, and feet. At each point, pause to notice any sensations—warmth, coolness, tightness, or relaxation.
4.   Release tension as you go:
As you bring awareness to each body part, if you notice any tension, visualize releasing it with your breath. Exhale and allow the tension to melt away. Don't force relaxation—simply focus on releasing any stress you notice.
5.   Finish at your feet:
Once you reach your feet, take a few moments to feel the entire body as a whole. Notice how you feel now compared to when you started. You might feel lighter, more relaxed, or simply more aware of your physical state.

The body scan is a useful practice before bed to promote relaxation, but it can also be done at any time of the day when you need to reconnect with your body and relieve tension.

Breath Awareness

Breath awareness is one of the simplest yet most effective mindfulness practices. By using your breath as an anchor to the present moment, you can cultivate a sense of calm and focus. This technique involves paying close attention to the natural rhythm of your breath without trying to control it.

How to Practice Breath Awareness:

1.   Get into a comfortable position:

Sit comfortably with your back straight, or lie down if you prefer. Close your eyes and take a few deep breaths to settle into your practice.

2.   Focus on your breath:

Bring your attention to your breath. Notice the sensation of air entering your nostrils, filling your lungs, and then leaving your body as you exhale. You don't need to change the way you're breathing—just observe it as it is.

3.   Use your breath as an anchor:

Each time your mind wanders, gently guide your attention back to the breath. It's natural for thoughts to arise, but instead of getting caught up in them, simply acknowledge the thought and return to your breathing.

4.Stay with the rhythm:

Continue to focus on the steady rhythm of your breath. You might find it helpful to mentally note "in" as you inhale and "out" as you exhale. This subtle labeling can keep your mind focused on the present moment.

Breath awareness is a powerful tool for calming the mind and body. Practicing it regularly helps to center your thoughts, reduce stress, and cultivate mindfulness in everyday activities.

Noting and Labeling

In mindfulness meditation, thoughts and emotions are often seen as distractions that pull you away from the present moment. However, the technique of noting and labeling allows you to observe these thoughts and feelings without judgment, recognizing them for what they are and gently releasing them.

How to Practice Noting and Labeling:

1.Begin in a relaxed position:

Sit or lie down comfortably. Close your eyes and take a few breaths to settle into the present moment.

2.Observe your thoughts and emotions:
As you meditate, thoughts, emotions, or physical sensations may arise. Instead of pushing them away or getting caught up in them, simply observe them with curiosity. Note what is happening in your mind.

3.Label your experiences:
Gently label the thought, feeling, or sensation. For example:

•If you have a thought, you might label it as "thinking."

•If you notice an emotion, you could label it as "anger," "anxiety," or "joy."

•If a physical sensation arises, such as discomfort or tension, simply label it as "sensation."

4.Let it go:
Once you've labeled the experience, return your focus to your breath or your point of meditation. By naming the experience, you create distance from it, allowing it to pass without getting caught up in it.

5.Practice non-judgment:
Remember that the purpose of this practice is not to analyze or change your thoughts and feelings, but to observe them with a sense of acceptance. Every experience is valid—there's no need to label anything as "good" or "bad."

Noting and labeling is a useful tool for breaking free from repetitive or intrusive thoughts. By recognizing and naming your mental and emotional experiences, you can prevent yourself from getting overwhelmed by them.

Loving-Kindness Meditation (Metta)

Loving-kindness meditation, also known as Metta, is a practice that focuses on cultivating compassion, both for yourself and for others. This meditation technique helps to foster a deep sense of empathy, kindness, and interconnectedness with the world around you. It's especially helpful for those who struggle with negative self-talk or have difficulty extending compassion to themselves or others.

How to Practice Loving-Kindness Meditation:

1.Find a comfortable position:
Sit comfortably and close your eyes. Take a few deep breaths to relax and center yourself.

2.Start with yourself:
Begin by directing loving-kindness toward yourself. Silently repeat phrases like:
- "May I be happy."
- "May I be healthy."
- "May I be safe."
- "May I live with ease."

As you repeat these phrases, try to feel genuine compassion and warmth for yourself. Picture yourself surrounded by love and kindness.

3.Extend loving-kindness to others:
Next, expand your focus to others. Start with someone you care about, such as a close friend or family member. Repeat the same phrases, but now direct them toward this person:
- "May you be happy."
- "May you be healthy."
- "May you be safe."
- "May you live with ease."

4.Move to neutral or challenging individuals:
After focusing on loved ones, extend your loving-kindness to someone neutral (like a colleague or neighbor) and even to someone you find challenging. The goal is to cultivate compassion for all beings, regardless of your relationship with them.

5.Expand to all beings:
Finally, send loving-kindness to all beings in the world. Imagine the entire world surrounded by warmth and compassion, and silently offer the same phrases to everyone.

Loving-kindness meditation is a heart-centered practice that can bring a deep sense of peace, connection, and compassion. It helps soften feelings of anger or resentment and fosters empathy for both yourself and others.

These four mindfulness meditation techniques—body scan, breath awareness, noting and labeling, and loving-kindness meditation—are powerful tools for cultivating a deeper sense of mindfulness, self-awareness, and compassion. As you explore each technique, you'll discover which resonates most with you and how these practices can enhance your overall well-being.

CHAPTER SIX

Overcoming Common Challenges in Meditating

Meditation is a practice that requires patience, persistence, and self-compassion. While the benefits are immense, many encounter common challenges along the way. In this chapter, we'll explore some of the most frequent obstacles and how to navigate them with ease.

Restlessness and Fidgeting

Restlessness is a common challenge, especially for beginners. The urge to move or adjust your position can be distracting, making it hard to settle into a meditative state. It's important to recognize that these sensations are natural and part of the process.

Techniques to manage restlessness:

1.Acknowledge and accept the discomfort: When you notice restlessness, bring your awareness to the sensation rather than immediately reacting to it. Name it: "This is restlessness." By acknowledging it, you're less likely to act on the impulse.

2.Body scan meditation: Practicing body scan techniques can help you tune into the body and its sensations without judgment. As you move your awareness from head to toe, you can recognize areas of tension and consciously relax them, reducing the urge to fidget.

3.Mindful movement before sitting: Sometimes the body simply needs to release energy. Engage in a few minutes of mindful movement before your meditation, such as yoga, stretching, or a brief walk. This can help reduce restlessness once you sit down to meditate.

4.Adjust your posture mindfully: If you truly need to move, do so with full awareness. Shift your position slowly and deliberately, keeping your attention on the sensations that arise as you move.

Intrusive Thoughts

It's entirely normal for thoughts to arise during meditation. In fact, expecting a blank mind can set you up for frustration. Instead, the goal is to observe thoughts without becoming entangled in them.

How to handle intrusive thoughts:

1.Recognize thoughts as temporary: Thoughts are like passing clouds—they come and go. When a thought arises, simply observe it without judgment. You can say to yourself, "This is just a thought," and then gently bring your focus back to your breath or the present moment.

2.Use an anchor: Having an anchor, such as your breath, a mantra, or a sensation in the body, can help you redirect your focus when thoughts arise. Each time a thought pulls you away, return to your chosen anchor without getting frustrated.

3.Don't judge the content of your thoughts: Sometimes, particularly intense or troubling thoughts may surface. Try not to judge or analyze them. Let them pass without attaching any significance to their presence during your meditation.

4.Be kind to yourself: Everyone experiences wandering thoughts, even seasoned meditators. Approach this experience with kindness and compassion, knowing that mindfulness is a practice, not perfection.

In today's fast-paced world, finding time for meditation can feel like a challenge. However, it's not about having hours to meditate but about creating consistent, mindful moments in your day.

Practical tips for squeezing in mindfulness:

1.Start small: Even just five minutes of meditation can make a difference. Begin with short sessions, and over time, you'll likely find ways to extend your practice as it becomes part of your routine.

2.Incorporate mindfulness into daily activities: You don't always need a dedicated meditation session. Practice mindfulness while brushing your teeth, drinking your morning coffee, or during a commute. By focusing on your breath or the sensations in your body, you can cultivate mindfulness throughout your day.

3.Set a regular time: Designate a specific time for meditation, whether it's first thing in the morning or right before bed. Making it part of your routine reduces the mental energy needed to "find" time each day.

4.Use guided meditations: Apps or online platforms offer short, guided meditations that fit into busy schedules. These can provide structure and encouragement to maintain your practice even when time is tight.

The benefits of meditation often develop gradually, and it's easy to feel impatient or frustrated when progress seems slow. However, impatience itself can be a valuable teacher in the practice.

Overcoming impatience and frustration:

1.Shift your perspective: Instead of focusing on results, try to view meditation as a process of self-discovery. Each session is an opportunity to learn more about your mind, regardless of how "successful" the meditation feels.

2.Let go of expectations: It's easy to expect immediate results, but mindfulness is about being present with whatever arises—whether it's a calm mind or a distracted one. Trust that over time, subtle shifts will happen, even if they aren't immediately apparent.

3.Practice patience as part of meditation: Patience is a key element of mindfulness. When impatience arises, recognize it, and gently bring your attention back to your breath. Use the experience of impatience as a tool to deepen your practice.

4.Celebrate small victories: Whether it's a moment of clarity or simply the fact that you showed up for your practice, acknowledge the small milestones. Progress in meditation is often subtle, and appreciating the little steps helps keep motivation alive.

Meditation is a journey, and like any journey, it comes with challenges. By addressing restlessness, intrusive thoughts, lack of time, and impatience with a mindful approach, you can move through these obstacles with grace. Remember, the goal is not to achieve perfection but to cultivate a sense of presence and self-compassion as you progress on this path. Each challenge is an opportunity to grow deeper in your practice.

CHAPTER SEVEN

Integrating Mindfulness into Daily Life

Mindfulness is more than just a seated practice; it's a way of living. By bringing mindful awareness to everyday activities, you can deepen your practice and enrich your life. This chapter explores how to incorporate mindfulness into daily routines like eating, walking, communicating, and navigating stressful situations.

Mindful Eating

Eating is often an automatic activity, done while distracted by screens or thoughts. Mindful eating, however, is about fully engaging with the experience of eating—savoring each bite, paying attention to the flavors, textures, and aromas, and listening to your body's hunger and fullness cues.
How to practice mindful eating:

1.Slow down: Begin by taking a moment before your meal to acknowledge the food in front of you. Notice its colors, shapes, and smells. Take a few deep breaths to settle your mind before you begin eating. This pause helps shift from mindless eating to a mindful experience.

2.Engage your senses: As you eat, focus on each bite. Notice the taste, texture, and temperature of the food. Chew slowly, savoring each flavor, and fully engage your senses in the experience. Pay attention to the sensations in your mouth and body as you eat.

3.Eat without distractions: Set aside time to eat without your phone, TV, or computer. Create a space where you can fully immerse yourself in the act of eating. Even if it's just one meal a day, try to eat in a quiet, distraction-free environment.

4.Listen to your body: Mindful eating involves paying attention to your body's hunger and satiety signals. Eat when you're hungry and stop when you feel satisfied, not when the plate is empty. This helps develop a more intuitive relationship with food.

Mindful Walking

Walking is another everyday activity that can be transformed into a mindfulness practice. By tuning into your body and surroundings, mindful walking becomes a powerful way to ground yourself in the present moment.

How to practice mindful walking:

1.Focus on your breath and body: As you walk, bring your attention to your breath and how it syncs with your steps. Notice the sensation of your feet touching the ground, the movement of your legs, and the rhythm of your body as it moves.

2.Be aware of your surroundings: As you walk, take in your surroundings with a sense of curiosity and openness. Notice the sounds, sights, and smells around you. Whether you're in nature or a busy urban area, observe what's happening in the present moment.

3.Walk slowly and intentionally: You don't need to rush. Slow down your pace and walk with intention. Feel each step and the way your body shifts weight. Walking meditation, where you focus solely on the process of walking, can be a valuable practice to integrate into daily life.

4.Let go of the destination: The purpose of mindful walking isn't about getting from one place to another. Instead, focus on the journey itself. Walk without the pressure of needing to arrive anywhere, and simply enjoy the act of walking mindfully.

Mindful Communication

Communication is a cornerstone of human connection, yet it's often rushed or superficial. Practicing mindful communication means being fully present in your conversations, listening without judgment, and responding with intention.

1.Listen fully: When someone is speaking, give them your full attention. Rather than thinking about how you'll respond, focus on their words, tone, and body language. Mindful listening creates deeper connections and allows you to better understand the other person.

2.Pause before responding: Before you respond, take a moment to pause. This brief pause helps you gather your thoughts, allowing you to respond thoughtfully rather than react impulsively. It creates space for a more meaningful exchange.

3.Speak with intention: When it's your turn to speak, do so with intention. Choose your words carefully and speak from a place of clarity and calmness. Be aware of your tone and how your words might affect the other person.

4.Be aware of your emotions: Notice how you feel during the conversation. If emotions like frustration or impatience arise, acknowledge them without letting them control your response. Practicing mindful communication involves staying grounded and emotionally aware.

Mindfulness in Stressful Situations

Stressful situations are inevitable, but mindfulness can help you navigate them with greater calm and clarity. By staying present and grounded, you can manage stress more effectively and respond rather than react to challenges.

Practical tips for staying mindful in stressful situations:

1.Pause and breathe: When stress hits, the first step is to pause and take a deep breath. This simple act of breathing deeply helps calm your nervous system and creates a moment of space between the stressful trigger and your reaction.

2.Observe your thoughts and emotions: Rather than getting caught up in the stress, step back and observe what's happening in your mind and body. Acknowledge the thoughts and emotions that arise without judgment. This helps you create distance from the stress, allowing you to respond more mindfully.

3.Use grounding techniques: Grounding yourself in the present moment can help reduce the intensity of stress. Focus on physical sensations, like your feet on the ground or your breath moving in and out of your body. These anchors help you stay connected to the here and now.

4.Respond, don't react: Mindfulness gives you the ability to respond to stressful situations with clarity. Rather than reacting impulsively, take time to consider your options. Choose a response that aligns with your values and the outcome you desire.

Mindfulness isn't just something you practice or a cushion or in silence—it can be woven into every aspect of your daily life. By bringing mindfulness to activities like eating, walking, communicating, and managing stress, you create more moments of presence, awareness, and peace. These small, mindful practices can profoundly impact your overall well-being and deepen your mindfulness journey.

CHAPTER EIGHT

Building a Mindful Lifestyle

As mindfulness becomes a more regular part of your life, the next step is to integrate it into your daily routines, work, and emotional responses. In this chapter, we'll explore how to develop mindful habits, enhance focus and productivity through mindfulness, and cultivate emotional balance.

Incorporating mindfulness into your daily life requires consistency and intention. By developing mindful habits, you can stay grounded, reduce stress, and find more joy in everyday moments.

Tips for incorporating mindfulness into daily routines:

1.Morning routine: Start your day with mindfulness. When you wake up, take a few deep breaths before getting out of bed. Set an intention for the day, such as staying present or being compassionate. You can also spend a few minutes in meditation to center yourself before the day's activities.

2.Mindfulness at work: Whether you have a desk job or a more active role, work is a great place to incorporate mindfulness. Practice taking mindful breaks—step away from your desk, stretch, and focus on your breath for a few moments. Before diving into a task, take a deep breath and focus on what you're about to do, letting go of distractions.

3.Evening wind-down: At the end of the day, use mindfulness to transition from work or daily activities to relaxation. Spend time reflecting on your day without judgment—just observe what went well and what you could improve. Consider a brief meditation session before bed to calm your mind and body for restful sleep.

4.Mindfulness in mundane tasks: Simple activities like brushing your teeth, washing dishes, or folding laundry can become moments of mindfulness. Focus on the sensations, movements, and your breathing while doing these tasks. Turning routine activities into mindful practices helps you stay present throughout the day.

Mindfulness for Focus and Productivity

Mindfulness isn't just about relaxation; it's also a powerful tool for improving focus, decision-making, and productivity. By training your mind to stay present, you can enhance your ability to concentrate and work more efficiently.

1.Single-tasking: Mindfulness helps you resist the urge to multitask, which often leads to scattered attention and lower productivity. Instead, focus on one task at a time. When your mind starts to wander, gently bring it back to the task at hand. This practice builds your concentration over time.

2.Mindful breaks: Taking short, mindful breaks throughout the day boosts productivity. Step away from your work for a few moments, close your eyes, and focus on your breathing. These breaks can help refresh your mind, reduce mental fatigue, and maintain steady productivity.

3.Decision-making clarity: Mindfulness helps you make better decisions by encouraging a calm, clear-headed approach. When you're faced with a decision, pause, take a few deep breaths, and allow your mind to settle before making a choice. This helps you consider your options more thoughtfully and reduces impulsive decisions.

4.Improving efficiency: By staying present and focused on the task at hand, you can work more efficiently. Mindfulness helps reduce distractions, allowing you to complete tasks with greater attention to detail. Over time, this leads to a more productive and fulfilling work experience.

Mindfulness for Emotional Balance

Emotions are a natural part of life, but they can sometimes lead to impulsive reactions or overwhelm. Mindfulness provides tools to observe your emotions without becoming controlled by them, fostering emotional balance and resilience.

1.Pause before reacting: When strong emotions arise, take a moment to pause. This pause gives you space to process what you're feeling without immediately reacting. Even a few deep breaths can help calm your nervous system and create a sense of emotional stability.

2.Label your emotions: Acknowledging and labeling your emotions can reduce their intensity. For example, if you're feeling angry or anxious, simply say to yourself, "This is anger" or "This is anxiety." Naming the emotion helps create distance between you and the feeling, making it easier to manage.

3.Observe without judgment: Mindfulness teaches you to observe your emotions without attaching labels like "good" or "bad." Instead of trying to suppress or avoid difficult emotions, allow them to exist without judgment. This acceptance can help reduce emotional resistance and increase emotional intelligence.

4.Respond with intention: Once you've observed and processed your emotions, you can respond mindfully rather than reacting impulsively. Ask yourself, "What is the most constructive way to respond?" Mindful responses are more aligned with your values and help maintain emotional balance in challenging situations.

Developing mindful habits, enhancing focus, and cultivating emotional balance are key to living a more mindful and fulfilling life. By incorporating mindfulness into daily routines, work, and emotional responses, you create a lifestyle that fosters peace, clarity, and resilience. These practices not only enhance your well-being but also empower you to navigate life's challenges with greater ease and awareness.

CHAPTER NINE

As your mindfulness and meditation journey continues, the focus shifts to building consistency, exploring more advanced techniques, and discovering new ways to deepen your practice. In this chapter, we will cover how to stay motivated in the long term, explore advanced meditation techniques, and discuss the benefits of group meditation and retreats.

Building Consistency

One of the biggest challenges in meditation is maintaining a regular practice over time. Life's demands can often interfere, but with the right strategies, you can stay committed and make meditation a lasting part of your life.

How to stay motivated and committed to a long-term meditation practice:

1.Set realistic goals: Start by setting small, attainable goals for your meditation practice. Instead of aiming for long, daily sessions right away, begin with just a few minutes each day. As your practice deepens, you can gradually extend the time. Setting realistic goals makes the practice sustainable and reduces the pressure to be "perfect."

2.Create a routine: Consistency is key. Establish a regular meditation time that fits into your schedule, whether it's first thing in the morning or before bed. Having a set time each day helps to build a habit, making it easier to stay on track.

3.Use reminders and prompts: Life can get busy, and meditation might slip your mind. Set reminders on your phone or leave visual prompts, such as a meditation cushion or journal, where you can see them. These cues will remind you to take a moment to practice.

4.Track your progress: Keeping a journal or logging your meditation sessions can help you see how far you've come. Write about how you feel after each session, any insights you've gained, or challenges you faced. Tracking your progress over time can motivate you to continue.

5.Be kind to yourself: There will be days when you miss your meditation practice, and that's okay. Rather than criticizing yourself, treat these moments with compassion. Remind yourself that meditation is a lifelong journey, and every day is a new opportunity to practice.

Exploring Advanced techniques

Once you've established a consistent meditation practice, you may want to explore deeper techniques that can further enhance your experience. These advanced practices allow for more profound introspection and spiritual growth.

Introduction to deeper meditative practices:

1.Mantra meditation: In mantra meditation, you repeat a word, phrase, or sound to help focus the mind and deepen your concentration. Common mantras include "Om" or phrases like "I am at peace." The repetition of the mantra helps to anchor your attention and can bring about a deeper state of inner calm.

2.Visualization meditation: This technique involves visualizing peaceful or empowering images to cultivate a sense of serenity or focus. You might imagine a calming place, such as a beach or forest, or visualize yourself achieving a specific goal. Visualization can enhance your mindfulness by engaging the power of imagination alongside breath and awareness.

3.Chakra meditation: Chakra meditation focuses on the body's energy centers, or chakras. The goal is to bring balance to these centers by directing awareness and breath to each chakra.

Starting from the base of the spine and moving up to the crown of the head, you visualize each chakra as a spinning wheel of energy, often associated with a specific color. This practice is used to promote spiritual healing and energy flow.

4.Loving-kindness meditation (Metta): Loving-kindness meditation focuses on cultivating compassion and kindness toward yourself and others. You silently repeat phrases such as "May I be happy, may I be healthy, may I live with ease," and gradually extend these wishes to others in your life, including loved ones, acquaintances, and even those you have difficulty with.

While meditation is often a solitary practice, meditating in groups or attending retreats can offer profound benefits. Group settings provide community support, shared energy, and opportunities for deeper exploration.

1.Community and accountability: Group meditation creates a sense of community and shared purpose. Meditating with others can offer motivation, encouragement, and accountability, making it easier to maintain a regular practice. The collective energy of a group can also enhance the depth of your experience, as you draw strength and focus from those around you.

2.Exposure to new techniques: In group settings or during retreats, you may be introduced to new meditation styles or approaches that you wouldn't have discovered on your own. Teachers or guides can provide valuable insights, share advanced techniques, and offer personalized guidance to deepen your practice.

3:Intensive practice in retreats: Meditation retreats offer a chance to immerse yourself fully in the practice, often away from the distractions of daily life. Retreats can range from a day to several weeks and provide an environment of silence, contemplation, and mindfulness. During a retreat, you may experience significant personal growth and gain a deeper understanding of yourself and your meditation practice.

4.Emotional and spiritual growth: Group meditation and retreats often lead to deeper emotional and spiritual breakthroughs. The shared experience of silence, reflection, and mindfulness can foster a sense of connection with others and the world. This collective experience can be transformative, helping you release emotional blockages and gain new perspectives.

Building a consistent meditation practice, exploring advanced techniques, and joining group meditations or retreats are powerful ways to deepen your mindfulness journey. With dedication, openness, and curiosity, you can unlock new layers of awareness, inner peace, and spiritual growth. Whether practicing alone or with others, your path in meditation will continue to evolve, offering you new insights and greater understanding of yourself and the world around you.

CHAPTER TEN

Embracing Mindfulness as a Way of Life

As you continue on your mindfulness journey, the practice evolves from isolated moments of awareness into a way of living. In this final chapter, we'll explore how mindfulness can transform your lifestyle, the long-term benefits for emotional resilience and mental clarity, and how it fosters spiritual growth and inner peace.

Mindful Living as a Lifestyle

Mindfulness doesn't need to be confined to formal meditation sessions; it can permeate every part of your daily life. By living mindfully, you can transform ordinary moments into opportunities for presence and awareness, creating a more harmonious and fulfilling life.

How mindfulness can transform not just moments, but entire ways of living:

1.Living with intentionality: Mindfulness invites you to bring conscious awareness to all your actions. Whether it's the way you eat, walk, speak, or work, you begin to live more intentionally, choosing how to engage with the world rather than reacting on autopilot. This intentionality brings clarity and purpose to your daily activities.

2.Cultivating gratitude and presence: By embracing mindfulness as a lifestyle, you learn to appreciate the present moment, no matter how mundane or routine it may seem. This fosters a deep sense of gratitude for simple pleasures, such as the warmth of the sun or the taste of food, transforming everyday experiences into meaningful moments.

3.Reducing stress and overwhelm: A mindful approach to life helps you manage stress more effectively. When you're present in the moment, you become less caught up in anxieties about the future or regrets about the past. This shift in perspective allows you to navigate challenges with greater ease and less emotional turmoil.

4.Deepening connections with others: Mindful living encourages more authentic and meaningful connections. By being fully present in conversations and relationships, you listen more deeply, respond more thoughtfully, and foster deeper bonds with those around you. This creates a more compassionate and empathetic approach to relationships.

Emotional Resilience and Mental Clarity

One of the most profound benefits of mindfulness is its long-term impact on emotional resilience and mental clarity. Over time, mindfulness rewires the brain, allowing you to respond to life's challenges with greater emotional stability and clearer thinking.

1.Strengthening emotional resilience: Mindfulness helps you build resilience by teaching you to observe emotions without becoming overwhelmed by them. Rather than reacting impulsively to anger, sadness, or frustration, you learn to create space between stimulus and response. This practice helps you process emotions more effectively and recover from setbacks with greater ease.

2.Regulating emotional responses: With regular mindfulness practice, you become more aware of your emotional triggers and patterns. This awareness allows you to consciously regulate your responses, preventing emotional outbursts or reactive behavior. Over time, mindfulness creates a more balanced and composed emotional landscape.

3.Enhancing mental clarity: Mindfulness sharpens your focus and clarity of thought. By training your mind to stay present, you reduce mental clutter and distractions, which in turn improves your ability to think clearly and make thoughtful decisions. This mental clarity extends to all areas of life, from work tasks to personal decisions.

4.Reducing anxiety and rumination: Mindfulness has been shown to reduce chronic stress, anxiety, and rumination. By grounding yourself in the present moment, you let go of unproductive mental loops and anxious thoughts about the future. This brings a sense of calm and stability to the mind, allowing for a clearer and more focused mental state.

Spiritual Growth and Inner Peace

For many, mindfulness becomes more than just a tool for mental and emotional well-being—it becomes a path to spiritual growth and inner peace. By cultivating mindfulness, you connect more deeply with your inner self and experience a profound sense of peace and unity with the world around you.

1.Awakening to your true self: Mindfulness encourages self-inquiry and introspection, helping you peel away the layers of ego, fear, and conditioning. As you practice mindfulness, you gain greater insight into your true nature, beyond the surface-level identities and roles you play. This journey inward fosters a deeper sense of self-awareness and spiritual awakening.

2.Experiencing interconnectedness: Mindfulness fosters a deep sense of connection with the world around you. By becoming more present, you realize the interconnectedness of all things—nature, people, and the universe. This realization can bring about a sense of spiritual unity and belonging, helping you feel more connected to something greater than yourself.

3.Cultivating inner peace: One of the greatest gifts of mindfulness is the profound sense of inner peace it cultivates. As you let go of attachment to outcomes, fears, and desires, you experience a deeper sense of contentment and equanimity. This inner peace is not dependent on external circumstances but arises from within as you learn to accept life as it is.

4.Spiritual growth through daily practice: Whether or not you follow a particular religious or spiritual tradition, mindfulness can serve as a bridge to deeper spiritual exploration. By continually returning to the present moment and cultivating qualities like compassion, gratitude, and non-judgment, mindfulness helps you grow spiritually and live in alignment with your higher self.

Mindful living is a transformative practice that affects every aspect of life, from daily routines to emotional resilience and spiritual growth. As you continue your mindfulness journey, you will find that its effects extend far beyond individual moments of awareness. Mindfulness becomes a way of living, offering a path to inner peace, emotional clarity, and a deeper connection to yourself and the world around you. By embracing mindfulness fully, you create a life filled with presence, purpose, and profound inner peace.

CONCLUSION

Embracing Mindfulness and Meditation for Life

As you reach the end of this journey through mindfulness and meditation, it's important to reflect on what you've learned and how these practices can continue to transform your life. Mindfulness and meditation are not just tools for relaxation; they offer a path to a more present, balanced, and meaningful way of living.

Embracing Mindfulness and Meditation for Life

Throughout this ebook, you've explored various techniques, challenges, and benefits of mindfulness and meditation. From overcoming common obstacles to integrating mindful habits into your daily routines, you've been introduced to a range of practices designed to deepen your awareness and foster personal growth.

The key takeaway is that mindfulness is not about perfection. It's about cultivating awareness, compassion, and acceptance in every moment. Meditation is a practice that evolves over time, and its benefits—emotional resilience, mental clarity, and spiritual growth— are experienced gradually.

Remember:

- •Consistency is key. Start small, stay committed, and watch your practice grow.
- •Mindfulness can be applied to every aspect of life. Whether eating, walking, working, or communicating, you can bring mindfulness into each moment.

•Patience is essential. The benefits of mindfulness and meditation unfold over time, so allow yourself the space to grow at your own pace.

As you continue this practice, you'll find that it becomes a foundation for living with intention, purpose, and peace.

Final Thoughts

Incorporating mindfulness and meditation into your daily life is a lifelong journey—one that leads to long-term well-being, emotional stability, and spiritual depth. It is an ongoing practice that requires patience, but the rewards are abundant. Mindfulness gives you the tools to live in the present moment, freeing you from the distractions and anxieties of modern life.

As you move forward, embrace mindfulness as both a practice and a way of life. Allow it to shape your interactions, guide your decisions, and cultivate peace in your heart.

In moments of challenge, return to your breath. In moments of joy, savor the present. This is your practice, and it will continue to grow with you as you evolve on your personal journey.

May your path be filled with presence, peace, and purpose as you embrace mindfulness and meditation for the rest of your life.

* 9 7 9 8 3 3 9 8 2 7 2 9 0 *